*letters to early street*

*Albert Flynn DeSilver*

# LETTERS TO EARLY STREET

La Alameda Press     Albuquerque

for Demian Yattaw
& to the memory of Carll Harrison DeSilver

Many thanks to Marian, forever in love and gratitude.
Many thanks to all who inspired this work, the infinite poetic and familial ancestors, and to all whose
words were "borrowed" in the great spirit of free lingual exchange. Thanks always to me mum, and
to Ajahn Jumnien, Dana Lomax, Paul Hoover, Bill Berkson, Anselm Berrigan, Edmund Berrigan, Alice
Notley, Adam DeGraff (wherever you are), Brendan Lorber, Lisa Jarnot, and Edwin Torres.

Many thanks to JB & Cirrelda at La Alameda Press for your kindness, patience, and great artistry!

*Pavement Saw* #9: Letter Two, Letter Twenty One; *www.Respiro.org*: Letter Thirty Two, Letter
Thirty Three, Letter Thirty Four (translated into Romanian by Alina Savin); *Slope*: Letter Three,
Letter Five, Letter Thirteen, Letter Forty Eight; *Poetry Kanto* (Japan) Spring/Summer 2001: Letter
Thirty One, Letter Twenty Nine; *Bombay Gin* Spring 2001: Letter Three; *The Wallace Stevens
Journal 2001*: Letter Nineteen (different version); *New American Writing #18*: Letter Nine,
Letter Twelve; *Hanging Loose* # 77: Letter Forty Seven; *Fourteen Hills Vol 6 No 1*: Letter One;
*Rhizome*: Letter Fifteen, Letter Nineteen, Letter Thirty Four; *Lungfull!* # 9: Letter Forty,
Letter Forty Two, Letter Forty Three, Letter Fifty One; *Tinfish* # 9: Letter Thirty;
*San Jose Manual of Style* # 3: Letter Twenty Five, Letter Thirty Seven, Letter Thirty Nine;
*Prosodia# 9*: Letter Thirty Six; *Skanky Possum* # 4: Letter Twenty Three, Letter Twenty Four;
*Big Bridge* Winter 2000: Letter Fifty Three; *6IX*: Letter Eleven; *Ixnay* # 4: Letter Four;
*Convolvulus* # 29: Letter Twenty Six; *Melancholy Breakfast*: Letter Thirty

Cover image: Paul Klee, *Legend of the Nile*, 1937
Pastel on cotton cloth mounted on burlap / Kunstmuseum: Bern, Switzerland

ISBN: 978-1-888809-50-3

Library of Congress Cataloging-in-Publication Data:

DeSilver, Albert Flynn.
Letters to Early Street / Albert Flynn DeSilver.
p. cm.
ISBN-13: 978-1-888809-50-3 (alk. paper)
1. Epistolary poetry, American. 1. Title.
PS3604.E7576L38 2007
811'.6--dc22

2007010590

Printed in Canada

La Alameda Press
9636 Guadalupe Trail NW
Albuquerque, New Mexico 87114

# CONTENTS

## LETTER ONE

Dear Demian,        this
               is not the first one or even the beginning—
Early Street doesn't have a when.
It doesn't begin, "Perhaps I shall practice being
dead to the world..." How dead to the world of
sensation, thought, idea is—I am not my idea
so perhaps I shall practice being
dead to the world—word, which is all idea, as one
practices knitting, guitar, medicine, or poetry
for that matter an unattached ecstatic
rather affectionately yours.
For Halloween I am spirit dressed up as matter,  dead
to the world of sensation (lank, bristling,
vacantly quenched).

I discover letter one will not escape
its singularity, the womb
looms always in my yearning.  This
is the thought I'm not and yet I write
with craving—a watershed, a womb, a wreath
of manzanita at my finger tips.  There is ink
in the wreath of manzanita scrawling
upon the clouds who blur up the sweat-drenched sun—

now just a pile of weepy ash defining the wind, masked
as your thinking, the womb.  So everyday I practice
this knitting with flame—ice-skate across eyeballs, strum
the double yellow lines, strung
across Early Street's dual-string asphalt guitar—
nurtured by this absence of when,
this song that reveals how it doesn't begin
or end with being dead to sensation's wind.

# LETTER TWO

Dear Letter Two,

I'll get to Early Street via twisting leg
hair into dark little conical
shapes on my thigh as a visual
apprentice to thinking.  Nerves
align in the same pattern in my brain.
Thirty seven orange cones
funneling us forward into a single
paginated lane.

It's just that you or I
can't see them feel, but we can feel
such shapes consisting of themselves,
we are consisting of ourselves, shapes
noodling along a rather lengthy road
of torque & vapor, the ceiling inside
the above unlimited, no longer an arrival
to anticipate in the world, its streets,
wheels, its bleeding directions.

## LETTER THREE

none begin, "Dear Whoosie..." Or filter you off into two
point perspective ironed to the horizon—a road
to meander alone—down a wet road steaming after the season's
first rain, leaves pulverized gorgeously to the pavement, their prints
I will mimic. We are led onto Early Street where
the yellow double line down the middle is a noodle
that strangles direction is a fat shoe lace high-wire untied
for clumsy ones with two feet and just when you've regained your horror
the asphalt dissolves and suddenly you are drenched in the sentence
we once reflected in those tiny post-rain pools—
gentle dishes set in the middle of your anticipation, the vertigo
is tremendous and lovely, is worn as a dress is your only display
besides the words pulsing by between sweaty toes on
the wire, the ripple, the yellow little clusters of energy passing
through the center of your direction—words throb. Now
there is a crowd of beggars with small nets in the whites of their eyes
their looking claims to catch your fall their voices scratch
the bottoms of your feet—the obvious next inclination is to
fall, the next inclination has fallen, reads, "Sincerely Albert" landing
words like little neon buoys landing in the blood words
bob in the body say, "The waking state is a hoax."

## LETTER FOUR

Dear I, Dear Deer,
        I will stray from one three
and two, in that order and revoke
all attributes that chain us
to the sequential, or ask us to follow
a similar node.  No ashes
are equipped with color—aren't they
parallel lineage and a phrase for the day?

My ears are planks waiting to happen.

For in the beginning it is found never ends,
the end ever ending is all fouled
up by flowering and the dead crust that follows.
Four lavender flowers on the cusp of a crack in
the middle of the earliest street I have ever
attempted, is just an old deer trail woven through
my thinking bleeds into the creases on my
forehead, capillaries thrashing in a furrow.

I will bundle the glorified brush me and deer,
us passing together through elemental thistle.

## LETTER FIVE

Here is a monument of wandering,
where it will take you no tooth can tell,
in your thought constructed boat
up that flooded avenue,
sponging flow to more gracefully vocalize your flesh.
The architecture of your articulations line the street
like babbling lampposts floating by
in which case you come to witness some artificial renderings
of being be
not alarmed for you are only a breath away
from the integrated whole—hold out not
no matter how svelte the thought, for example;
"if death blots black out, must then blink light in"
Where the form of a white gust arrives
as a relief effort sewn
in a honeycomb cloud pattern the sky
weaves forth from what?
Being is then shed from these masses of air
and curls up in a crystalline ball
for all to rejoice around and speak at as if
you were addressing some mystical oracle
that turns out to be the sunburned back
of your neighbor's head
shining brightly through the hedges.

# LETTER SIX

Began with some noxious mentation
yesterday hard-pressed to the pavement
yet buttered itself by heading out to Point Reyes.

Warm November, fried oysters, a pair of screaming gulls
between bread my head now bent
against the sun's dying reflection on the sea.

I'd like to traipse out on that shimmer
like in some of the older poems,
but the shimmer has been cut short, doesn't

quite meet the horizon anymore,
goes only about 9/10ths of the way out, ten
degrees to the right of the Farallon Islands.

3000 miles from Early Street this season wondering
if I walked that solar plank on liquid foot
how I'd land on the dock at Early Street's Atlantic end

and you'd be there with your arms gasping, breath
outstretched through firm air, at sunset, eyes sleeved
in red flame blinking against our disbelief, brief
skeletal selves.

## LETTER SEVEN

Is lost within the luck an ox hauls.
Is the word-dug space between shallow

hands.  I am not this letter, this ox, nor
the road-crux that ink tills, hauling

vein scrawl across the bleak-
leaking whites of a gathering eye.

Early Street is a place fuming with candor
where soon you will have to face so quietly

you, stewing in your own juices.  Remember, a star
in the sky that you can't see, sees you

for all of what you aren't, nothing (wisdom)
and all of what you are, everything (love).

## LETTER EIGHT

Dear air,

        I will never forget how being saturated
in your declarations keeps me expansive & meanderable—
the ephemerality of letters staked out in the clouds,
our felt gown in flames, the orange one I wear here on earth
breathing forth multiple enigmas twice a moment. Winds
are the first powers to be addressed in any ceremony.
It only seems fitting for without,
our lungs would shrivel—
hello hollow income whole I borrow
space—O great permeable one, breathe out
here on the page between lines, would you? I
will step aside, I will go away, I
will become uninvasive in the air above Early Street.
How those winds at our finger tips hold us to the sky.
Such luminosity is within the general sweep of heart
that comes uncontested with a deep breath.

## LETTER NINE

I can't believe we're all gonna die here
in this sentence.  I mean we just got started
weaving funny nerves.  I've never really even been here there
and amn't I always writing from a point of disbelief?
I have a fact to grind, where
willingly I tear my silhouette down,
right in the midst of the community nerve garden
harvesting the narrow wisp.
Time here is treated like a bullfight, time.
It's rough being time, isn't it not so—
stop complaining O perpetual one!

I feel like a dinosaur already born within an inevitable extinction
and having to read about it everyday is exhausting, and trying.
Trying shovels.  Some where some, this is a letter, dear you this is filled
with too many 'ands' & 'I s'
I went to the beach and became sunny and said,

"footprints are out to spell"

and meant it.  Words were sanded before me there
in little divots between winds, where all is forgiven,

all is for giving sandy words and unsanded ones
to whomever towards & withever which
we rough up the world.

## LETTER TEN

The sun is at this exquisite angle
and my head fits it.
So I'll see ducks flutter under fold & blink.
I'm fine sand on warm or and…
Today the reflection seas upon them,
peels off the surface and smacks
me in the face,  however gently—
I am warmed by this and the
fine sand being porous air, how it
loves & pours into us here.

A gull uncaps the wind, sea-
weed ribbons toward.

While thumb-sized skittering plovers crowd
tide line in, then chase foamly, streaked undertow out.
All this on a pair of small dishes
at the backs of my eyes filtered
through some gorgeous receptive
arrangements firing spontaneously;
a prism flowering forward
for me to meet it.

## LETTER ELEVEN

is a  lament
is lame cement is
rendered under water
from this morning's steady rains.
Keeping my eyes sealed in bed
they are drowning in their seeing, but
of memory        memory swells.

Each organ is wrapped in a claw
of thought, gasps at the scene—

the heart for example, or is it my heart as example
resembles the width of a wet loaf of bread
scrunched to the size and shape of a fist—
ready to punch red water, ready
to punch its own weight.

Braids in the water spoken if by plumes
where standing at the river bottom
crows shower a puddle via reflection
their feathers usher the ripples onward, crumple.

Early Street is late for seeing,
my vision is a tease to feeling.

# LETTER TWELVE

Dear you who where or when is not
you'll love this when I'm dead
for when I'm dead will be then love.
My raining aria you aren't anymore
besides the wrecked tractor-like sadness I sense
as well a vague lump in the progression.
My clouds ache and throb backwards
they are communicating at an unknown rate—
meanwhile impermanence is going up on trial
even in the midst of its burning a single tear
which is launched off my cheek and lands
with a sizzle in the middle of her speech.
I will drown within its teaching
and drown of all approaches to a malnourished
yearning, blurring the yellow parallel—
Early Street was never two ways.


How traumatically escalated
& beamingly sufferable life really was
and though I never got to ride a giraffe
through downtown Omaha, or
canoe into fjords for pennies a day,

I felt wealthy among the combustions and steady
in the wake of anticipated dreams, those
who pressurize sexually against us.
No matter how tight within the feather-vein
we get, our attachments will strangle
till we unweave for love.

## LETTER THIRTEEN

Dear You,

now is your time to fondle the lightning
like the sturdy nutrients of solitude
quietly imbibing.  Since incomprehension

is after all being alone.
Alone,    who is al-one?

Why do you not think of you as the coming one—
is it for being caught missing our turbid communion?

We people err so often in the air
and then land in the tentacles of some less loud.

Life has become intolerable without your olives—
my heart has unswervingly atrophied here, hence
the love of all my intimacies, must be let go.

## LETTER FOURTEEN

Dear Madhattan,
     Today I enter your dented thigh island
and bump my head atop silver block letters:
"DEPARTMENT OF WEL ARE."
The 'F' has been stolen, the 'F' is alone
it hath fallen off its brick facade—
if only well we were and didn't
need your dismembered letters
this mid-December.

Signs are acts of assertion are themselves uncertain.
See the blank page to my left?  Open wider.

Semi-green leaves are still handing branches
to New York's crisp sky line, like reason
forever nondescript or even linear I
can't believe the sun warms at such a lazy angle.
Can Early Street be entered at this angle?
The air is slanted to my skin
at 42°.  I am canyoneering with the rays
down Amsterdam Avenue, I will ride
their lances and lance up a bagel
at Barney Greengrass' zoftig nest.

Hans Memling's pretty boys have followed
me down from the Met.  There were men
shoveling chairs who now crowd
the 3 train with muscular stares—
one in particular is holding his heart-
shaped prayer book, and another with pale
face, smudged beard, and eyes lit curious
brown, is straightening his thorny crown.
The pinks of his eyes are disturbingly true,
they are fine examples of grace etched with rage
blurridly contorting all figures seen—
they say, "grief is a window that pines"
and, "loneliness is a habit that we're encrusted to"

## LETTER FIFTEEN

Dear speaking of lines,
        some should just hang em up to dry!
I figure if *it* doesn't have metal-hemmed Daffodils
or an oniony muscle, then it ain't worth the ink it takes
to fake out a vacuum.  I'm talking about gorgeous
distorting simplicity, such that fans your graceful stupor—
yanks bland sparks into clever flames
till the haptic space of the screen chars,
and reels in the smoke of transparent convention.

## LETTER SIXTEEN

Dear —

Our existence becomes the vertigo
of a ceaseless mutability.
Where drawing breath is punctuated
by golden drops sprinkled through episodes
of greenish names, arid scarves,
ferocious dresses found in our mute
abandon to merest breathing.

Our afterward is befriended by a found calm
inhaling each river we flower through
we are flooded, silently abundant in a watchful mind.
Like prose, these waters are plurality or
a bud in a pond proceeding the word—
my shifting lunar essence leaks like
moonlight through the slats of an old barn at dawn.

*Our ritual gestures are self-sufficient in their meaning.*

Heat within the mind incubates experience
the way a white Christmas satisfies tradition—
the dreadful and the delicate surfacing

together in pairs indifferent to their
projections and perceptions
of one another, they settle into being,
yet cling to breath like how a wet
snow clings to these wrought iron railings,
the balcony I lean over,

72nd street New York City
breezy, 34°.

## LETTER SEVENTEEN

Dear Wallace,

moonrise at sunset is
the same moonset

at sunrise is who
I see me in an aspect of.

*The Palm At The End Of The Mind* is taped to the windshield,
taped to this desert landscape, taped to eastern Oregon,
taped to the Owyhee River we just rode over on
the wrong side of the road dreaming
of baboons and periwinkles.
Reading while writing while driving while Wallace—
I'll crash into idle roadside planets and
gawk at what shape these stars have carved us into!
And in the same breath be buckled in thought
when I see forget-me-nots
grow wild in the corners of your smile—
your smile is
but a thousand miles away in
some inflatable city by the sea—
and I grow liquid missing this
and how you've forgotten mine—

mine smile.
It is reflective of those sculpting stars
like I've told you
you are, but the further I drive the farther you go, the
less meaning the memory—
*as evening dies in the bodies' green going.*

## LETTER EIGHTEEN

Dear Whatever—
I can't seem to just let em pour—
the words, that is
like trains pouring by
arattlin' rather crookedly
this morning they hammer
the tracks in some gunshot fashion.
First the 5:18, then the 6:18, then the 6:50
A.M. something—am what?
An occasional horn wisping by?

Being unearthed here on the banks of the Hudson
of what accords are unaccounted for—
the weather right now is so exhaustingly
uneventful I'm ready to just placate
flatly against desire.  For awhile the clouds,
fatigued in their mispositionings, are itchy
orange smudges who tend to dandy
up one corner of the sky, the only corner
worth standing under.

To feel weighted by this day and its absence
of participation or is it precipitation?  I need

to precipitate bodily against this day
with a little more lurch and swizzle, inflict
more spice upon today's doldrums, lay
nakedly pooled for silent
& skinny rhythms.

## LETTER NINETEEN

Without disposable thumbs
I wouldn't stand a chance on my hands.
Except at the landfill where I could go
awinnowing through all the other
discarded necessities
and bless each cast out note these
words decomposed upon ignition
where utterance is left in its length
a gray shutter & a cough
sputtering through dirt that is treated
like dirt.

What if the letter O was treated
like a seed?  The sound of a shape of a sound.
Whatever else might be said, for example

    —bloom—

a simple and profound miracle
thrown away.

## LETTER TWENTY

Dear leaden clouds O leading where,
how can we light up
anything early with such
a cavernous & weighty
pupil-cast shadow?
How do you expect the poem to sun?
Early Street is fresh out of footing—
see how the day peels back
its gray lid, in which a 4 call crow
does so 7 times, checks into
my ever widening ears.  Intervening
as she does so brightly by hearing.
The wash of traffic washes
over my skin, all signature
to this arrival, a soaked January
dawn.  For breakfast I'll eat a bowl
of yellowfin tuna, then
with abandon jerk off into
numbness in the corner
of this round room
discovering that another one of my
coined terms is headless,
doesn't pay.  So then, back off
the page, go back to sleep, see

a bruised stone reinflate
in the wake of an aeon, notice
that her tongue's horizon
is lined with violins
& find how one thought
gets another thought
caught in its throat.

## LETTER TWENTY ONE

Dear level angel, be astonished!
Feel blessed by the words that disintegrate
Before your very mouth.

This morning Chopin fit an etude between my oat flakes.
My ears salivated all over the flowers.
True moments surrender under an allegiance to fire.
This is the opposite bewilderment that decorates
My place of sleep—

A stuffed moose has just capsized in my bed.
It is a charming wreck of fur & wonder—
The low-eyed constellation from which I grow
Where Early Street once clearly stood.

The alphabet is shattered across the shattered asphalt,
Is a brittle and unwatered direction wide open—

Love, in a state
Of flesh-lucid confusion.

## LETTER TWENTY TWO

Dear There,
        There is an air
stained with disappearance—
where we are force-fed the
amplitude of vacant circumstance.
There, is an occasion
spanning the roots of an astute
abandon.

I love you more than the sprawl of veins!

High-lit between the whites of oceanic eyes,
we but two shirts who've past in the night
now just a castle of moonlight and sand
left to set sail
upon my wavering hand.

Memory flowers with an intent to diminish—
and so I'm on the prowl for such disappearance!

I'm on the prowl!
I'm off the prowl!
I'm on again off again
prowl!

Won't you have me over for a glimmer?
Adam will and says, "To complain, just means
to write poetry." He is misquoted and I am complaining,
although we'd rather be snivelling
under a green umbrella while
splashing at our absence
with a loosening strife.

## LETTER TWENTY THREE

Dear Edmund,
       How'd you get the history of the human body
to fit into a poem, when I can barely get a one
lane road paved with letters?

Yesterday I saw a bruised stone reinflate in the wake
of an aeon—it was gorgeously inviting, so I entered.
I spread the word & was questioned and was answered.
My friend said go to the shrink.
So instead I went to the stuffed moose, and then to
the doctor who said, "Open your wallet and say ahhhhh."
He reached in and found my tongue in the wallet
and a set of sharp teeth that bit his greasy hand.
With the greasy doctor's hand still in my mouth
I went to a bar and told this exquisitely sexy woman
that her tongue's horizon was lined with violins.
She spit her martini in my face, and the olive landed
in the doctor's hand.  So I went home and wept and
wrote it down, wrote it all down that one lane road.

# LETTER TWENTY FOUR

My air eyes are
Seeing vicious beauty swallow sparrow
Camped out in "The Letters" trembling dawn, dreams
Of a fading gray Connecticut.
I once lived in a Clock Tower with bats in the belfry
Like frantic winged pupils of the eye
It is not towering now but drowning
The thinning Housatonic carries it to Sound
Its knotted watery twine on fire
To swim in burned droplets, memory therein
Wet sparks as if the aftermath is ashen thought
Which it is, Sunday's ash beginning to sing
From out warm hands Early Street was born—
My path breath-strangled
Against a cantaloupe moon.

# LETTER TWENTY FIVE

Dear mid February dawn—
        it's morning in the Headlands
in the sky,  she said, in the sky where
we were basted, in a little torn piece of it,
sky, so swollen blue.
I fell in of with err and
suffered an immaculate orange
trough.  An immaculate orange
trough the tankers are pasted
against the horizon, like small cities
drifting out to sea, where a cluster of my
celebrated thoughts     bob—
church bells on the choppy surface.
War batteries wander, crumble off
worn out soils.
A man takes a picture and is halved—
the landscape suffers a minor misreading
eventually takes its picture back.
Slam of waves through rock
spouts brushes air's knots out
like how all my exiting lovers
leave me Neruda,
nude and sputtering at the snowy moon.

I have a hankering for women with a wind chill
here's where I repeatedly swoon.
I think of all the frivolous tremblings
because of my them of. I've
fallen in of with err yet again
in the mist of this letter, is it eleven?
Letter Eleven from the Headlands, the one with
asphalt ripples, this morning's rolling ocean skin.
This is # 25.
Numbers are chasms with hats.
I want to cradle that frigid lava peeled
from the Golden Gate and placed in my eye.
It is smeared in a way,
in a tasty way to my eye's tongue,
my tongue's eye seeing apricot
spreadable fruit, breakfast in the Headlands,
good morning.

## LETTER TWENTY SIX

Dear San Francisco,
                floating down Montgomery
I find the TransAmerica building being pulled
flat against the pointed fog, and watch
a sex-confused side street wet itself.
It is ashamed, it blushes gray from embarrassment,
and then floods an alley to the eleventh floor.
So I follow a different block
paddling my wicker canoe through
lofty blood pillars at the Old Fed.

Ahh to move within the city of the pinstripe
vortex, you who knot up men into furious circuits.
To stroll beneath a cardboard skyline & bypass
high-heels clicking against foreign polished granite,
a forest of aimless hollow stockings.
Where are the legs? Oh buoyant metropolis,
show us your shapely legs,
all spent and crinkled in an awkward gallop.
Are you running from your own
claustrophobic bulk?
Have you been chased away

by executives with vexed cuticles
who claw at reduced air?

Such moments here are as sturdy as a held breath.
The sun is my pencil sketching limp shadow.
It realigns billboards into abstract petroglyphs.

Picture ancient Babble.

Ask the men with cement ties held around
their wax necks, they look like unpotted plants
who have surrendered to being parched.
I hear sirens cup their spark-crusted mouths
while uninformed men in uniform
confiscate their dying.

## LETTER TWENTY SEVEN

Dear emptiness,
      The other day I let my burst heart
sack of blood lilies spill
while reading *Siddhartha*
in the parking lot of Lucky's.
The universe was all sprawled
out upsidedown on the back of my retina
like skunk meat on the freeway.
Each face on the street turned into a slice of bread.
In terrified hysterical laughter I phoned several
numb ears while watching my tears cartwheel
into heavy traffic. They were run over, they
didn't mind. My mind had taken off its trousers
and was standing half-naked in a phone booth. My mind
was shimmering in the run over tears shimmering
in one numb ear on the other end. The ear turned
into a fistful of silver trillium,
the phone booth a shimmering casket
in which I was carted off
into some brilliant green star.

## LETTER TWENTY EIGHT

Dear Early Street, dear darkening ground,
      The text of your unfolding
     is written in our walking.
     Your path is urban boulevard
     and deer trail all the same—
     where taxicab and insect
     segment intersect.
     This road is the unread
     word of our wandering—
     each distance breeds a deeper
     solitude, each curve a meeting
     with ourselves.

## LETTER TWENTY NINE

Dear great swelling Pacific,

    Today I fall asleep before your quivering upper lip
upon a single grain of sand.
It is the one grain less slept upon.
From there I watch the reflection of a clear
wiggly capillary skirt a blank stone.
It turns out to be a cellophane leech
feeding off my seeing.  I name him dissolve.
We go walking hand in eye, eye in hand
down the beach where it begins to rain—
I get trapped in a drop and then leap off
into buoyancy questioning its impermanence.
It evaporates in my face (the drop) does, like a slap
and says, "evaporation is an imposition!"
Agreeing so in blue air I fondle a pudgy gull
with my outstretched eye,
Early Street shifting beneath that single grain of sand.

# LETTER THIRTY

Dear Stone,

I feel your billion year old Agrillitic heart tick hard
into one damp palm.  What a wonder time
bringing you here from the suave Mohave
into this thin hand of shadowed awe.

I see your stiff face accurately drawn
with premonitions of landscapes & beings
yet to come.  Who knows of what
colors then by now; pupil depth
black drops, tough mauves, charred orange
rust reds, delicate desert browns all woven
together via threads of lit silver.  Articulations
of color drawn with fire:
A 17th century Japanese seascape woodcut print,
a decaying Redwood snag, the silhouette
of a man standing agaze in the soft desert dawn.

Over a billion years drawn this
floral matrix of chemistry—fire spoken
into stone the hand of lightning sketching
our future visions, time sucked out of itself

transparent against the mirror of creation
burning ancient presence——eye
to air & back these great costumes of fire we wear.

## LETTER THIRTY ONE

Dear etc.,
What fluttering currents shriek out of steaming pores
We dying all the while via maddened flame
My frail oars part timid waters in a teacup
Hours ripple up a dappled shore
An indented chin is upon the dented page
E-mail from Albania went dark
"...end up raped, with no parts of body
          like the massacred ones"
I was born crying, I shall die laughing—
My wishful thinking peels back
At dusk the black surface
Of a pond from it's darkness, I
Wear it as cape; black liquid flight
Upon my neck.  Sunrise in the rising
Valleys of America, safe in the costumes
Of production, our products are our pillows—
Weeping willow, weeping products, weeping
Darkness, weeping body parts out of out-
Turned eyes.  Oh the rain drop bird riffs
I get dropped through this
Mourning the mix and Spring's scratch
Of black ink against obliterated petals, etc.

## LETTER THIRTY TWO

Dear you, past path,
        The garden of my memory is sprinkled with
landmines kissing tulip petals—do tiptoe with caution
and keep the frozen glow on your chin pointed skyward—
yellow up the cloud bottoms if you will.
I will when as a child I was convinced buttercups were
painted with butter, margarine rather, it was the late 70s
margarine was more yellow plastic flower. Now my chin
is forever Connecticut and as for the rest of my head, go walking.
I can't even remember how dicey are flowers
especially etched in tepid circumstance. I heard classical
Vietnamese music this morning before the 6:17, between rain drop
bird riffs ended up raped and I through the window of those sounds,
awoke, grabbed ink around the neck and started bloodletting in response
to having stood on the wrong petal. The garden of my memory is
obliterated petals who left only this weakened scratch of black ink.

## LETTER THIRTY THREE

Dear Demian,
      These last few letters are trying
Too hard toward capsule—poems
In the small town where I live.
Brash, unexpected, compellingly floral—
A roadside vendor selling double yellow lines through
Either of two layers of white matter in the cerebrum.
I can't decide which to take
With me into this next life
Either of two, or neither of both,
Which fit in a compact detachable receptacle
Bound for the Persian Gulf.
I love you more than the sprawl of veins.
These lit birds here make a glad land.
I can hear the music of her tears
From across the freeway the Adriatic sea.
Early Street has run this way—
The repetitive pronoun is loose on the small town
Where I live killing certain unwalked dogs—
On the same street where Henry Vaughn sheds his fleshly dress,
It's 1650, no it's 1999—complete with no parts of body
Like the massacred ones.
Why does the word sacred inhabit massacred?

Wits are impatient insects
In the small town where I live.
And this on me one lettered breath
*Let me die before my death.*

# LETTER THIRTY FOUR

Dear me,
       I sometimes forget that we are
inside of outerspace.  Just because the earth
has become overly familiar to us we seem
to have this blade forgetting.

Often I have to peel back my green skin
and remember certain ooze.

It says in his letter how information
is overrated, how it masks up the incisions
we have driven into wisdom.

Yesterday I spent three hundred and sixteen dollars
and twenty seven cents and was awarded
a caramelized ham.  It fit in the dark sandal,
so I walked it home.  At home the cats
were wrestling doorknobs, dogs doors
havin' a hoedown,  down in the underworld,
in outerspace on the overly
familiar farm I live in a
kind of self adhesive
closure am closing in
upon its outer
walls.

## LETTER THIRTY FIVE

Dear Tracy,
          These are not letters are rather
where witherers frolic upon loss.
Early Street is an inside job. As in a fist-
sized job. You know the one, the throbbing
red rumbling one. Where the vanishing point
comes into view, where two fucking black & blue
butterflies have landed, to feed off my heart in the Headlands—
which I am all for, and so I watch them intently
fucking upsidedown on a single leaf of grass my heart
blown lanky in a thick gust     hanging
on for dear life, literally hanging
just so, in a cold jerk wind
off the spun-blaze horizon.

The other day on my way to work, ten days
prior to the fucking butterflies I saw a sign that
said my gasoline purchase helps fight child abuse.
I broke down crying in the breakdown lane
and kept driving shoulder to shoulder with my self on the shoulder
wishing I was one of those fucking butterflies, (feeding
off some lank heart in the Headlands). They just are
no matter what, as we should be but aren't

due to all of our thought-constructed boats.  I should speak
for myself and my own armada.  One boat now
in the foreground has a Post-It note pinned to its
sail which reads, "there I was in love anticipating
the nostalgia that was about to ensue."
Off it flutters into my missing of you
and how we used to act, beautiful
like those fucking inscrutable
black & blue butterflies.

## LETTER THIRTY SIX

Dear grief, one bird
            my clunky temple—
I climb your split clouds
and discover brilliant wings—
skin-up-step wings
step up crisp into sculptured stone
wings    who were swept
thin over the waning
page    where skin and I wept
gracefully through Thursday's rain—
this rain was said wisdom from a raven;
("...take this body into your dying...")
Arms tear soaked and waving
against cheeks    we
one bird grieving into our disbelief
brief skeletal selves.

## LETTER THIRTY SEVEN

Dear 37,
you are the most commonly random
number known to man.
You comes up over and over again
and furthermore repeatedly.
You're one of those hatless chasms
that I have spoken of—
one of the few.  One,
is the other one—
supple         convenient        bald.
A number that charts vacancy's bucolic spread,
An emptiness worth sinking into

the only hospitable vapor I know
& love
& trust.

## LETTER THIRTY EIGHT

Dear Demian,
      I miss you & your pen
& your pal who was washed
through the streaked panes
of a dead man's eyes—
who was then wafted up
into that circle of sparrows
coiling up a glass-rimmed
sky.

Forest Knolls is full of its
forested knolls—the 116 year old
Korean man makes a killing selling 40s
to the Harley crew across the street—
Literally a killing selling,
from the tumble down
Little Store on the corner, he
should be selling rural
rustic charm to the yuppies
rather than 40s to the Harleys.
Here come them frigid spring
shrouds of Pacific fog punctured
by sonic motorcycle thunder, their

echoes spilling over Bolinas ridge—
I'll curl into one like a pine-top burrito &
become gray, become sway!

## LETTER THIRTY NINE

Dear Tracy,
        Hello—It is 5:38 in the morning
in the year of the big shirt.
I am not my idea.
This refrigerator is a freight train
in my basement dwelling—
I write to you from beneath the rails.
Toast & butter & apricot spreadable fruit
is a sign that I am coming.
My dream a frozen shovel
void of letters, my dream being trapped
in plummeting aircraft. The citizenry today
is a single dead halo, dragging
flocks of thought across their day.
Here is where a tattered whale rears up
on its hind legs, and speaks against
the pre-waking Pacific dawn:
"Dear you who where or when is not
you'll love this when I'm dead for when I'm dead
will be then love."

# LETTER FORTY

Dear Sincerely Albert,
         You are my sacred nerve cartographer
reinflate my trampled map si vous plait
help me navigate my way into interior ways
untangle my respectfully submitted veins from
around the whipping post, wood you?
Horrific filament sprawl of this kind is
terrific—don't say terrific, it's oversaid in these certain
terrific circles.  See what I mean?  Hey, any idea how to steer
this thing          this body          this circle, dear me
I am not my eye, ear, either—I lease this body
with an option to buy.

Me lank of frame today, steering my antique camel,
I mean, carriage, blind into overly familiar galaxies
banging headlong into galaxy X.  Hello galaxy X
so nice to see you!  How is galaxy Y?
It's April 24th in galaxy X.  Exit galaxies.  Press enter.
Enter Early Street, O marvelous body of my green going!
I love you however awkward in your erratic gallop, gallop on
spring phrasings, on into, The Watershed, where I was having a word
with some little angel Douglas Iris flowers, some
were faded, were lavender & birded
one was wan canary.  Their words were petal swipes
of prayers, prayers my cartographer ironed from nerves.

## LETTER FORTY ONE

To & After Hart Crane

Dear Hart,
        I write to you from beneath the ocean
Where bird spread lachrymal flocks take flight
Through a love dense rinsing of the moon
Dissolving all but windows from the mill,
Here square water curdles this unyielding smile—
Whitely names are peeling from mine eyes,
Letters who spell out in palm, sketch pain
Show their undimming lattice work of flames.

Betrayed stones speak beneath the echo tendoned loam
Lifted up in lilac emerald breath
The grail of earth again!

My face from charred & riven stakes
Near bent from grief this still
An unmangled target smile is rising
A swift floral loft from the ripe borages of death
Clear my tongue!

For immaculate venom binds the fox's teeth
And swart thorns freshen on the years first blood,

Like twanged scarlet primrose, trillion on the hill
Where red tears of inaudible whistle
Are tunnelling song.

# LETTER FORTY TWO

"Questioning means taking the road to despair...
    ...true knowledge is daily awareness that, in the end, one learns nothing..."
                        —*Edmond Jabes*

Dear despair,
          we live for now
in the late April rain
on an empty hollow street
on a limp & vacant ribbon
washed away from this water
in a country of fragile boundaries—
the houses that line this washed away
street are really countries waiting
to sever any entry.  And they do,
like our knowing, can't help it, water
has carved & carried us singly into the weakened
shape of a private meanderer            walking
blood-lost through no house drowning
in no country.

## LETTER FORTY THREE

Dear equivalence,

I can feel a letter
welling up from that massive

fathom at the cusp
of what breath borders

upon hesitant
heights, here

where my absences
are all up to spec.

Soon this letter will shed its dilemma,
like an exasperated lemon-cloud—

Then the diehard physicalists
will have to absorb

the difficulty of such spendy
ephemera.  How I enter

endless confrontation with no
emblem but skin.

What more want do you want from a street,
but a clusterfuck of stars at the keyhole?

I'm applying to be a resident
of a place I already am—

equivalent to a mastery of presence,
my original legitimate habitat

is surrender.

## LETTER FORTY FOUR

Dear Letter Forty Four,
        Look at all these voluptuous
thoughts flushed through the continuous
present. They're sprockety, low cost, voiceless
thoughts, blur into one vast
thousandfold thought. Where you uncurl
out of tangible lamplight
where my body gets amped by your olive skin
which ceases to exist before
my nerve snarled eye——
the idea of you leaving,
leaves fly off
the thought about tree.

We have six billion years till
the sun becomes a white dwarf. I personally have
much less time am already a white dwarf with beaming
yellow habits. Life is just a hyper
extended errand, so what's all the fuss about fact about,
its all pretty extinguishable anyway. See above       leaves.
See what I mean you mean he means she means they mean it means
sky. Please feel free to talk amongst yourselves    sky.
Gone is a misnomer for resonant vapor.
That guttural first syllable diminishes into its ensuing fumes    gone.

Then what?  Presence doesn't need a parking sticker
does it?   A wicker flagship that crickets the wind?
It's nice to wake up and watch sensation spool
off soft bone into such well behaved
twilit light.  Enchantment today
is the only discipline.

# LETTER FORTY FIVE

Dear Poem,
      When are you gonna shape up
and become thrillingly brilliant to the general
reader—contemplative to the temporary ear?
Begin by addressing general reader with respect via
astute vacuity.  Early Street, each sheet is a blank
star,  is a blank stare, is canceling nothingness;
a nest stretched from the center—L'etoille—
"we are our road"

I'm in Paris at the Arc de Triomphe, no I'm in New York
at the stifled fringes of desire.

"To write is to seek a permanent confrontation with death"
Yikes! I'd rather have an iced tea and walk up Lexington Avenue
in the middle of a June day, & enjoy the women being consumed
in their own humidity;  "Hey, there's wildman on unicorn"
they shriek, out the window of the Frick.
I love how I evaporate in the midst of their faces
as they cascade into me, and how I cease to exist
in the light of their beaming, whether brutally or beautifully—
I am there, I become their stunning dissolve.

## LETTER FORTY SIX

Dear Brendan,
        my, what a splendid
bookshelf you have! Today was charcoal
in New York. Many women swam
in my eyes and left charcoal pebbles
for pupils. I felt gifted, drenched,
then blinded by them. But swarms
of pelicans came out, and filled in the
blanks, swept my heart off a pulp rug—
where some teeth sprung up like sharp
oceanic blossoms. I am a sharp oceanic
blossom, rowing through the dying plates
of daylight. I am not my idea,
do you hear me? I refuse
this noodle and the eye it nooses.

Was once unarmed upon entering, became
unlegged upon exiting, yet upbeat &
twangy I rode on, saw depths in bricks,
and counted the beaks of demented
sparrows out your window. Where ever
my vapor flowers, is good. I recognize
its shape at once, even here in the past.

Dear Brendan, may we bake bread
in your brick oven bookshelves, read
for a wee bit in your 4th street window?

## LETTER FORTY SEVEN

Dear Marian,
          These thoughts after rain
stir green yellow pollen, make it swirl upon a puddle—
Wet sidewalks dry from the cracks and edges
Inward.  I like the way your eyes enunciate
such shreds of lettuce light.  Speaking of eyes, I have little bits of
speech in mine,  "say, I'd like to see you again,
*after a while*"—Which after all is more blurry,
yours or mine?  I'd like to see you again,
again—before this *after* is over, in Nirvana
for example, though Nirvana makes me nervous.
I'm scared of heights, or is it space?
Heightened spaces, or them spaced-out heights
above Central Park South.
The Saag Panir in your teeth
got me all riled up, up even further
than goat milk curdles.  I'd like to hold your hand
above the curdled goat milk, pinch the east
& west coasts' together, I dream of a 3000
mile long hand, it smiles like how only
a hand can smile.

## LETTER FORTY EIGHT

Dear Marian,
　　　　I wanted to say, not nearly
as such, but didn't out of fear.  Instead
said, "I'm a rainbow dust matrix,
a flustered angular particle,
a nothing in particular kind of guy."

Am I still a swell, or a swollen vortex in your eye?
Does it matter?  Am I even matter?  Is matter overrated?

Your charm and sweetness isn't, it's electric,
yogic, terrific!  My thinking you into
oblivion, a gorgeous wing I'd like to sleep within
this poem nor the others are a letter
after all—all of the nothing that we're fond
of knowing, & our ideas about each other—

leaves fly off
the thought about tree.

## LETTER FORTY NINE

Dear Marian,
        The fog has slipped in over night
gently smearing the tree top's dark green heads,  gray.
As I am busy smearing thoughts of *Sleeping on the Wing* across the page.
I wish I were a sleepy bird not heavily flanked by reason
clarity, or even mimicry which is native to bird being.
Going into the world as into the air as into the page,  an
incorruptible ghost ship adrift and in defiance
of physicality so fucking temporary, empirical——Haaah!
You know my atmospheres are just thin dresses, red
wind permeable garb.  I let you in, we mingle, swap vapors,
kiss each other's vastness, and are gone.

# LETTER FIFTY

Dear Marian,

      Today I wake feeling nude & stupid
which I take to be an improvement over clothed & knowing.
I & me in the cloth are my evil twins—
I dispose of them at once. Then I fill
an envelope with a fragile, limited edition,
endangered ecosystem. It fits nicely in a # 10 I send
to you in midtown Manhattan. I immediately feel
prompt, courteous, and dependable. The postman disagrees, says
writing 'FRAGILE' on the envelope is crying wolf,
so I bite him in the leg.

I'm already nostalgic for my anticipations.
This feels like a crutch for exiting presence—
Is being clever such an accomplishment
for our naked, hairy, accomplishment
bodies, or just mere convenience for the eulogist?

I'm addicted to acting out of body. So much for
turnstiles and timetables—a pile of rose petals
on the paisley table is my desk. Such a despondent wolf I am
scuttling off with a mess of bills, letters, & postal pant legs
in my mouth.

You called to say your cat ate one of the written upon
illegible petals I sent you in that # 10.
Which one was it?
Histrionic, anticipatorily, yours, love, Al—
any or all of the above?

"Burp...          Meow" says the cat.

## LETTER FIFTY ONE

"either you are body conscious and a slave
of circumstance, or you are universal consciousness
itself and in full control of every event"


Dear mind,
        mind flora mind fauna, sprawl
                as you may this June
Where P. Whalen is
        disguised here          as


            HORSEFLY


    on my foot!   He neighs
and gallops off onto the foot of Taos Mt.


            Sun warming early cool,      creek
        shuffs by,        no shuffles, by      yes    shuffles—


There goes the reflection of shuffling water pooled in a lawn chair
rippling on the banister, me coasting on the duck, I meant deck—


        "feeling ducky"

New Mexico gives me a feeling inside,
of canyony pinyon piney vast bird breaths SCREECHING
                                        beautifully by & by


                    ducks & elephants trodding about in my abdomen.


Control is vandalized in the belly by a herd of elephants
                        a hunger gurgle?  A stampede of missing?


                    DUCKSCATTER!


    What colossal, lumbering elephant-thick
nerves we have for breakfast today,
                        raking over the New Mexican plain—


                        abdomen as savanna.


            See what thoughts do, they


    FAN THE GUT,


                    rake the plain.


Saw antelope off 64 West do the same—

                    yet at this time
                            crickets start their clicking
early in the tall morning                grass              between Pinyons
            breakfast is served in the EAR, AIR, OUR bird

has 2% wing fat to go
with the 2% milk fat in the fridge,
                    low fat milky bird.




                              *




I'm in full control of this noodle—nobody move!

My seeing is its command,

                    Cottonwood tufts drift by like so,
                    snowing from nowhere
                    into my hair, snowing
                    heavily now, now heavenly
                    against the bright blue June
                    sky, where I act just like snow

flakes, a control freak?  An un-
attached ecstatic one, none
the less,  melting in the sounds

of

wind chime,

stuck flies,

spent wingz exhausted

at the window like my thinking

is, just so,

I'll sit silent
ly then,
and listen

to the sun        yawn.

# LETTER FIFTY TWO

Dear Alice & Doug,

　　Last night I dreamt 'we' had a slumber party at rue des
Messageries, at a timeshare condo in Vermont in rural France. The
walls were glued grains of rice and unsoaked legumes in pale
unfortunate earth tone colors. They were spread out on the walls in
obnoxious designs. There were sleeping bags everywhere strewn in
the orange shag carpet. There was Will, Eddie, Anselm, you two, Noel
who was hovering, and Adam who played this translucent spirit number
milling about in the curtains. Your bedroom was the size of a rec-room,
it was a wreck, we were all invited in. Downstairs the air was a smog
of cigarette/pot smoke and water vapor from the kitchen sink. There
were dishes there, we had had pasta for twenty even though we were
8. Outside was gray and unsettled weather wise. The dream was lit by
a perpetual barely emerging dawn, both inside and out rolling hills of
pine. Out in the parking lot my friend Marian was grumbling beneath
a bicycle, a bit peeved at having to ride her bike home several thousand
miles across the continental French Vermont United States. I was
uneasy about waking, I had never gone to sleep. I reached for my book
on the bedside table and in response to your recent reader inquiry, (as
to the features of a new poetry movement) wrote:

　　torque, vapor, and heart, the ceiling inside unlimited—should be chubby on
　　spirit—humble, honest, full of egotistical lies, wrought with contrarianism,
　　like real life—should be absurd in a lovely and emotional way. One should

be enchantingly baffled on a regular basis. Should be should free—
have a "grumpy and harassed irony"—include "the largest male detainee
population in the free world" in proportion to the largest free female
population in the detained world. Include the animals, minerals, molecules,
and spirituals. Be lank, bristling, vacantly quenched and ultimately
complete with several different flavored dwarves.


With love & owls in the esophagus,

Albert

# LETTER FIFTY THREE

Dear Anselm,

It's 8:41 in Forest Knolls on the 25th of July
in the year of the big flustered shirt. I am drowning
in polka dotted comforters and scotch flannel crosshatchings.
The ecstasy of grieving is the one free thing worth spending.
And so I'm thrifty with it and the days
who do not flip by like pages have rather
become the flipping. That teetering wheelbarrow
full of blood is perched on the bookstack
at the foot of my bed, there are occasional
spills in the sheets when I reach for a word.

I read Frank's *Joe's Jacket* and think of Adam
in a seersucker suit en route to nirvana (a sheet of blood
veiling the entrance) acting as seer aching to suck
on some young girl's ear. Has he skipped town on the swami?
Is he now swimming through Colorado on a freight train?
The continuous present continues to presently go away.
This makes me feel grumpy and harassed
so I scratch at my bloody sheets at my cheek
which got caught in a violent dream last night
its interior a ball of newly chewed gum.
This the vicious elegance of presence, presence
being so revered these accelerated days—

is time being shoved into a speedier gear?
How can we know its not just our seeming—
because it seems as if our knowing
is just an over stated moan.

## LETTER FIFTY FOUR

Dear Demian,  this
is not the last one or even the beginning
Early Street doesn't have an end
or even a when—
for all the pulpy tundra's teeth are agape
with gaps.  Snow drifts in
between them teeth to the heated mouth.
Where in the beginning it is found never ends,
the end ever ending is all busied & bruised—
I find me to be my own brazen druid acolyte
one minute picking blueberries
in the Schwangunks, the next spasmodically thriving
off the absence of actuality.
I am equipped with more facades
than a fake mining town.
There is a fake mining town
roaming around in my head right now.
I feel I must change my bonnet mid nod,
now I nod off often into exotic war zones—
the wars in the papers are an erogenous zone.

I am in love with all of the above
I am in love with the 'it' of "it's raining"

you in the muggy midst, my nights of thin sleep
scant trains, midtown canyon thunderstorms—
each sheet between us is a blank star
our love, it bleats in silver carbonated blots
I feel closer to you, my angelic blank star
as affectionately detached as a well fed cat.

Presence as condiment—my face against the window
feeding off the able blend
of morning light on 49th street.
Robins and sparrows in the sumac trees
between brick buildings,
a two call crow and a Skil saw—
I must be in the country the city the same
elusive thing—here where my dying
elders embers are, my darlings
we busy sponging the receding light
where the thoughts foam up
and disperse at once, and I
into a born-again invertebrate ink spot,
a great floral stain
on the pulpy tundra's teeth.
I smile as only a hand can smile,
with these letters in hand, in tooth

on my way to the post box, the hat box,
the box of rain on the stoop
overflowing with this song of how it doesn't begin
or end with being married to sensation's wind.

# COLOPHON

Set in *Goudy Modern*, a design originally cut in 1918
by Frederic W. Goudy at his Village Press & Letter Foundry.
Monotype released a version in 1928 which found a popularity
lasting for decades. Its rhythmic informality may or may not
be modern, yet, as Goudy said, reflects "… an intangible
quality of freedom." With long serifs, small x-height &
ascenders taller than capitals, what moves on the page
is an interplay of black notes & white spaces like a
solo by Bix Beiderbecke—quirky, elegant & astute.

Titling: MISPROJECT / Eduardo Recife

*Book design :: JB Bryan*

Albert Flynn DeSilver is a poet, teacher, visual artist & publisher living in Woodacre, California. He received a BFA in photography from the University of Colorado, & an MFA in New Genres from the San Francisco Art Institute. He is the author of many books & chapbooks including most recently *Walking Tooth & Cloud* (French Connection Press, 2006) & *Some Nature* (The Non-Existent Press, 2004). His poems have appeared in dozens of literary journals worldwide including *Zyzzyva, New American Writing, Jacket, Poetry Kanto, Van Gogh's Ear, Hanging Loose, Exquisite Corpse,* & many others. He is also the editor & publisher of The Owl Press, publishing innovative poetry & poetic collaboration. He teaches workshops in writing, poetry, and publishing throughout the San Francisco Bay Area and beyond.